SLIM CONFESSIONS
THE UNIVERSE AS
A SPIDER OR SPIT

Book Cover Art: "Loss" by Miles Johnston. Used with
permission of the artist.
Book Cover Design: Sarah Minor & Sarah Gzemski
Book Interior Design: Sarah Gzemski

Published by Noemi Press, Inc. A Nonprofit Literary
Organization.
www.noemipress.org.

SLIM CONFESSIONS
THE UNIVERSE AS
A SPIDER OR SPIT

sarah minor

"For academic men to be happy, the universe would have to take shape. All of philosophy has no other goal: it is a matter of giving a frock coat to what is … a mathematical frock coat. On the other hand, affirming that the universe resembles nothing and is only formless amounts to saying that the universe is something like a spider or spit."

—Georges Bataille, from "Formless"

"FORM IS NEVER MORE THAN AN EXTENSION OF CONTENT."

—Charles Olson [via Robert Creeley], from "Projective Verse"

"The stuff streaming word-by-word across the lines dripping down the page of my notebook."

—Eileen Myles, "Everyday Barf"

This book was written between July 2017 and December 2018 in the Norðorland Vestra and Vestfirðir regions of Iceland, and in the states of Vermont and Ohio, USA.

For SH and CA

The Icelandic word for lamb is "lamb" but the village where I climb down from a tall, hot bus is called "Hvammstangi," and I'll never learn to pronounce it quite right. There are six dogs on the farm, nine people, and three-hundred sheep. It is early summer, lambing time. A season of cold fog when the collective body of the flock crowds indoors for two months of constant birthing. Each morning I push two layers of socks into a pair of borrowed skateboard shoes whose laces have dried beneath a cake of manure and placenta and whatever else. Out the barn door stands a glacier and not one tree before the horizon. There is the moss and algae of Iceland—long and flaxen in streams where hot spring meets snow melt to comb plants across miles of crusted lichen. Everything out there that should be green is grey. Elsewhere, in other times, I've been a waitress, a maid, a shift manager, a cabaret's secretary, a research assistant, a gardener, a ghostwriter, a tutor, a baker, a floor model, a gift-wrapper, a caterer, a wood-fire maker, a nanny, a set painter, but never have I spent this many consecutive hours touching something live.

In 1970 the artist Robert Rauschenberg presented a piece titled "Mud Muse," a rectangular glass trough containing formless, grey-brown material that some called "listening mud." As Rauschenberg's "synthetic, primeval slime" bubbled and flowed, its burbles and sluices activated a nearby sound system, which recorded the ambient noises of the piece and played them on a loop that activated air jets beneath the mud. The material triggered the recording. The recording reanimated the material. And when "Mud Muse" opened at the MOMA, the audience reacted to it physically. Thinking the silky mud was natural, they dipped their hands into the tank. They used it to paint the gallery walls. Some visitors even tried to climb into the trough and bathe in it. Rauschenberg and his scientists were concerned about the body's tolerance of the material because it was made using Bentonite, still a relatively new chemical at the time.

In the opening shot of this video, a Youtuber sits down in a mini dress. She crosses and uncrosses her left knee. She crosses and uncrosses her right knee and her elastic hem pulls shorter. She tugs the hem down, scooches back in her seat, and repeats this sequence twenty times. The camera zooms in as her thighs make soft exchanges and her lap changes its nature. When she's finished she'll turn at an angle to demonstrate the column of horizontal slits cut into the right side of her dress. She'll lift her elbow and use her right hand to pluck the rungs of fabric that ladder from hip to armpit, watching the camera. Then the other side. Then she'll offer advice the way a pretty older sister might, sometimes saying "daring," and often the word "commando," but always, eventually, she says, "This is how you do a sliming." Though more often, lately, she'll say "take" instead. A man in plain clothes steps in, always from the left, and his head gets cut off by the frame. She'll tense a moment as he dumps the heavy bucket over her, but then she'll tilt her head back and open her arms, as if taking in the wind.

ACCOUNT OF A GELATINOUS METEOR: Adams, Ellen M. and Schlesinger, Frank. *Nature Magazine*. 84: 105-106, 1910. "Dear Professor Schlesinger, --- Referring to the falling meteor of which my husband made mention at your lecture last evening, the facts are as follows. One evening, some years since my father Mr. Joel Powers, while walking on Lawrence St., Lowell, Massachusetts, saw a brilliant shooting star or meteor flash downward through the atmosphere, striking the earth quite near him [sic]. He found it upon investigation to be a jelly-like mass, and almost intolerably offensive in smell. I have often heard my father allude to this event, which greatly interested him, he being a close observer and an extensive reader. Respectfully yours, Ellen M. Adams."

It's June in Iceland and cold enough that breaths are rising from the pens. I practice moving toe-heel down the wooden aisles that double as feeding troughs, scanning the wooly backs. Farmer Ivan leads the way, stopping to point out the signs. How one sheep directs her chin to the rafters through a strain. Before this she bared her teeth. Before that she huffed, quit chewing her hay. He shows me how to read the barn, because the births here happen in cycles. Soon, before I'm ready, labor will spread through the flock imperceptibly, the way contractions ripple the skin beneath a fleece. First one ewe will call out, then another, shouting across the barn, and at my feet will be a third one screaming. Soon, we will be running between stalls with no time to redden our hands in hot water. There's no soap. Then the quiet. Everyone lives. Birth is gory and dangerous, even for the hearty Icelandic sheep, and each pair of lambs is precious for its market price—the reason farmers like Ivan have been living on an island the texture of a Brillo pad for nine generations. I first arrived in this country as a researcher on a grant to study the way language attaches to a landscape. I came for bones and books and origins, for translators and linguists. The cheap, yellow apartment I rented belonged to my father's college friend, Sven, who picked me up from the airport in Reykjavìk and pulled over on the way to make another copy of his key. He showed me the slender apartment that had been his mother's—a kitchen, a bathroom, a bedroom, a balcony—and then sat down on the couch and told me to take a bath and lie down for a nap. "I will wait here," he said. We spoke different languages. "Thank you,"I told him, "but I'm trying to wait out the jetlag." The conversation repeated itself. Then he shrugged and took me out for groceries and a router. On the car stereo, Sven played house music he'd produced at a national studio while we drove across the port city and back for a calling card. Back in the apartment, he unloaded the paper grocery bags and then set both hands on my shoulders. He turned my body away from his to face the bedroom and walked me through the open door. He was older than my father and—I could feel it—frailer, too. Standing beside the bed, he said, "You lie down for a nap." I wasn't ready when he began to grope me, so I was already saying, "No thank you." Then I walked myself back out into the foyer, and in thirty seconds he had said goodbye and left with the master key. I sat down where before I had stood on the floor. Afterwards, I spent my first three weeks in Iceland moving on busses between the yellow apartment and the national library, between a sulfurous faucet and a rolling cart with green felt shelves. I touched what I was allowed. Then I woke one morning, climbed into a hot bus, and didn't step off the ring road until it shied from the northwest peninsula. I opened the door of an Icelandic sedan and the Chihuahua in the passenger seat moved over for me. The farmer's wife, Katrina, stopped at the store for chicken cutlets and then drove us out to an expanse where the sun sank below the horizon for only three hours a day. North. No cell service. One shower every three days, though none of this was in my grant proposal. Mornings, I zip on a parka and walk to the barn where, in the next hour, five Icelandic sheep will try to become mothers. Those of us on two legs will play the game of *guess who*. Farmer Ivan doesn't speak any English, but he makes good jokes with his hands and has never brushed against me. Instead he stops with one hand caught on the wooden railing. "Slím" he says, pointing to a ewe with her face in the corner. I widen my eyes at him. "Slím" he says in my direction, his sore knees giving into a squat. I copy the stance and look beneath the railing where a rope of white snot is descending from the antisocial sheep. Her rearmost source blows a pale bubble, as with a wad of cheap gum. "Slime?" I ask. The farmer repeats, lengthening his vowel, and elaborates, "now the lamb comes." In this way I learn that, before the slick twins, before the horns, before the front comes out the back, slime announces a beginning, and also a version of the end.

1969, Five pm on the southern edge of Lake Erie. A red squirrel—not fat, but lean—darts between a buckeye and a fresh trash heap and works its jaw around a corn chip. The moon at the back of the sky and the moon in the oiled river are setting brackets around this, the afternoon of Cleveland's thirteenth river fire. At the top of the buckeye, a spider is working her six spinnerets, laying fine lines that conduct electrical current and bear more tensile strength than steel. The rail tracks along the bank collect heat, and a horn sends our squirrel back up the tree. The spider breathes, or rather, a hot wind moves through her. Something like a hubcap is shining between the rails, and though the wheels are slow to come they send up a comet of orange lights that scatter into the river, or into "a sluice of debris," "an oil slick," "an island of sludge," that newspapers will later report. It smolders. Then the surface ignites; the river is on fire. The flames are five stories high.

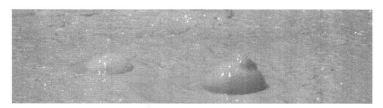

In 1990, Nickelodeon star Lori Beth Denberg, who acted in shows like *All That* and *Figure It Out*, recommended that, while getting slimed, a participant should always lean backwards. Otherwise the slime is likely to shoot down the back of their pants. Denberg added that the green of Nick's slime stained, and that the color could not be washed out of pale bras and underwear. The slime, even in her retelling, still gets the last word, a double punchline, a cue to the audience to laugh and applaud.

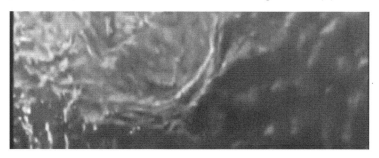

1994, my parents' damp basement. The living room

carpet has followed the staircase and the green lacquer railing down to a TV set where the secret pudding recipe is making a curtain of some contestant's hair. Applause spreads through the screen like static. I'm in my regular seat on the rug with gooseflesh strung along my arms, unwilling to leave the TV glow to find a sweater. I make my own applause with a new toy—a plastic sleeve filled glittery, purple gel—by hopping it from one cold palm to the next. I was born into the era of Gak and Squand. The time of Tacky Hands, of Gooey Looey and The Ooze, of Gushers and Flubber and Floam (*the fun you can feel!*), in the days when slime was becoming a regular verb but still before we had the language for "screentime." Back then slime was a new narrative scaffolding, the arc of gameshows and cartoons structured around its release. Now it is 2018, and slime is making a return. This is the year *You Can't Do That on Television* gets its reboot. This is the year I turn thirty and become addicted to Instagram, a platform where the new "Slimer" community thrives. A cycle is the opportunity to recognize patterns. A chance to adapt. Slime is a texture, a noun turned verb through screens. My interest is in this—slime that travels—how a material becomes narrative once it encounters human skin.

#slímconfession: The first time I worked on a sheep farm, I arrived on foot with a college boyfriend just days after the high-walled truck had carried the newest generation of lambs off for processing. At first we couldn't pronounce *Llanidloes*, but it was there I learned how to bottle feed a runt, and there that he learned why counting sheep is no joke. We didn't know what we'd missed—where all the other lambs had gone. In the hayloft it was so cold that we slept together for warmth, head-to-toe in a narrow single mattress, in hats and sweaters, so cold we learned how easy it was to pull another person's pants off from that angle, so cold that for a month, with the smell of the animals on us, we only touched each other with our mouths, lying that way.

"The basic phenomenon has been seen the same since written history began. A meteor is seen to land nearby, investigation reveals a jelly-like mass in the approximate location, thus we have 'star jelly' or, more scientifically, a 'gelatinous meteor'" (*Handbook of Unusual Natural Phenomena*, 1977). In his medical writings, John of Gaddesden mentions stella terrae (Latin for "star of the earth" or "earth star"), "a certain mucilaginous substance lying upon the earth" and suggests that it might be used to treat abscesses.

The Slime-a-Thon charity project was a precursor to the Ice Bucket Challenge of 2012. Early on, its participants blended a second YouTube genre, the "Outfit of the Day," with slime buckets as parody. Those videos of girls slimed in OOTD mini dresses garnered larger audiences and longer comment threads. The perfect outfit, erased. Somewhere along the way, a body contour dress designed by Nickelodeon star Victoria Justice, with a ladder-like slit up the side, got specifically involved—and there was born the variant YouTube video genre "How to Take a Sliming." Almost every user who makes and posts these videos rehearses the same script. "Some girls cover their faces," the performer will boast. "You see other girls looking down and bending their head forward," and "wiping their eyes." "But not me" she'll say, "I'll show you how you do a sliming," "this is how you take it right," as if a different choreography can give women power over a material, a narrative of their impact and not the other way around.

In the 1953 film *It Came from Outer Space*, slime was a one-eyed extraterrestrial trying to flee planet Earth. Five years later slime played its first villain when *The Blob* began consuming entire crowds on screen. Its single eye began to revolve the following year when slime landed in a flying saucer in *Atomic Submarine* and chased spacemen away from *The Angry Red Planet*. The X-Men found slime working as a sideshow act in 1964 and a year later it fed again on crowds and sewer chemicals while a frantic cast tried to keep *The Clone* out of Lake Michigan—slime was expanding its color scheme, and taking people with it. Then, in 1970, it was cast briefly as a friendly, shapeshifting cartoon the shade of Pepto-Bismol in the children's book "Barbapapa" ("Cotton Candy"), and then the first official, kid-friendly TV sliming came in '79 during the pilot episode of *You Can't Do That on Television*. By '84, as the laugh track was at its peak, slime took up the role of punchline as it textured the sets of *Ghostbusters* (ectoprojection) and played "Slimer"—a fart incarnate— during the era when it first became a verb. Then in '87 a meteorite landed in a rural lake and, one-by-one, slime plucked teenagers from *The Raft*. In '88, Nickelodeon introduced Nick Jr., and Sly Sludge and The Ooze terrorized the planeteers on *Captain Planet*, and slime rode the Enterprise as Evo. Then slime went silver and metallic in *Terminator 2* and *Alex Mac*. It jived in *Flubber*. It was sold in several textures, as "Squand" and "Gak," and licked paperback covers in the Goosebumps series below titles like *Monster Blood, The Blob that Ate Everyone,* and *The Horror of Camp Jellyjam*. The return of slime accompanying a cartoon villain (working for "Toxic. Inc.") showed up between '70s comic books and early '90s cartoons like *Captain Planet*, which marked the reaches of an early environmentalism focused on visible pollution. In TV shows that snuck sticky green Aesops into children's programming, scientists were often villains, or at least were clearly labeled "bad" or "good" scientists.

Long before he built "Mud Muse," Robert Rauschenberg was raised in Texas, near the oil fields ringed with pits of leftover Bentonite, a clay-like substance known as "drilling mud," that softened into a sluice when the pits gathered rain.

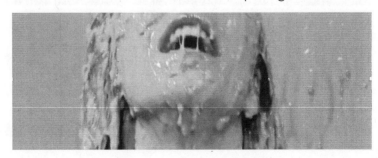

After a week in the barn as Ivan's apprentice, the farmer leaves me in the care of Birgitta, an Icelandic girl who is much younger and taller than me but who has perfect birthing hands. Birgitta's skipping school, where she learned her English, to work on a farm for the season. Under her work boots, she wears rainbow knee socks, reads horse-girl books, wants to be a midwife to *persons* when she grows up. Birgitta tells me that I need to cut my nails as short as they'll go. She teaches me all that Ivan hasn't: how to bottle feed the orphaned lambs and curl them through soft rings in a basket beneath the heat lamp, how to fold my thumb against my palm to slide five knuckles into a ewe's vulva and then the birth canal, how to wrap up all my hair in a scarf, like she does, so it won't leave my pillow smelling bad. The farmers set me up in a bedroom that used to be a closet before they added a plate glass window as tall as the ceiling and pushed a bed beneath. A bed in my room means that the wooden door opens just wide enough for my body to pass sideways, and I like it this way. Just a thin, white shade and a bed in a tank of light. All my life I've kept a plant where I sleep, and here in Iceland it's a pile of yellow-grey moss pulled from the field and resting in a paper plate on the sill. Nothing that comes from this place needs much else to keep it going. Every day after work, Katrina turns the Wi-Fi on for two hours. Then dinner, then reading, then sleeping through the midnight sun. Birgitta spends her two hours swiping vertically on a smartphone with nails that are hard-stained black at the edges. In another week, my hands will match. Days, there are the animals, our hands inside the animals, our tired backs, the sodden barn. Nights, there is the tank of light, the screens with our hands at the back, and once per week, the big wall-mounted flat screen plays *E.T.*, Birgitta's favorite, with Icelandic subtitles. Inside the farmhouse the dogs are Chihuahuas. They eat hamburger and salted fish and sometimes a kibble brand called "barking heads," and they rarely get set down. Outside, in the barn, the dogs are Icelandic sheepdogs. I don't know what they get fed or when, but I've seen them eating from the dead lamb barrel, dragging a small one around until its leg is a bone. Their job is to loll tongues in the corner until a live one gets loose from its stall. My job is to bottle feed sheep the size of rabbits, to remember who has two or three, to work tiny hooves out from floor slats, to stare at vulvas, reach in up to my elbows and find a shoulder blade, to fill pill bottles and water troughs, and all this for the slaughter. When this one comes, she'll land with a slap and make way for her brother. Her flanks will steam, and so will my hands when I hook a finger past her tongue to lay it down. Had I known birth was yellow? Placenta silver? And there was the time when I didn't know lanolin—wool grease, sheep secretions. Now every day I open the barn door, and I can feel it hit my eyes. After an hour, the smells subsume me, and all I sense is hay warming in sunlight like soft dough, the salty steam from the waterspout routing the hot spring to the sink, and the sound of three-hundred sheep in slow labor. At five p.m. Birgitta and I walk silently up the long road to the farmhouse. On the couch, we hold our smartphones close to our mouths and pass a beer to the coffee table rather than between our hands. Our arms are numb-tired, but every so often Birgitta turns her phone out to face me, and I pull her hand closer to watch the subgenre she's teaching me to love. "Touching by looking" is what some are calling it. The visceral image. The modern "Slimer" community is vast and made up mostly of kids who use hands-free webcams and microphones to film homemade "slimes" in lavender and chartreuse and baby blue. These users gather in the comment sections of Instagram videos that feature pairs of hands manipulating homemade "slime" to produce effects like "the sticky crunch" or "the thwock," sounds that mimic crumpled notepaper, bubble wrap, or a jar of damp pebbles, stirred. The Slimer community is mostly preteens and younger, but as users of screens since infancy, the group has already recognized the specific conventions of the videos their peers will seek out. This season it's become our ritual to watch slimes after long days of a different texture. Some of the Slimers go as far to describe the scents of their slimes in the captions below. Vanilla or bubblegum, lemon or apple. "SLAP IT," pleads the first comment beneath a smooth, kiwi-scented slime on Birgitta's screen. "Do you know what this means?" I ask her, pointing, and she only nods, doesn't look at me.

In 2018 playing with slime on camera involves a strict choreography within the online Slimer community, who communally regulate the means of teasing sound from a material that grows denser as it's worked. A slime video lasts no more than a minute. The Slimer reveals nothing but their hands. The slime comes out of a clear package—the kind users can order from Slime stars who make the viscous material in a range of textures and sell it via digital platforms. In popular videos, a Slimer will pry the lid from a container and unstick her material from the walls by plucking it with one finger, moving in a circle, folding the slime into a ball. Then she'll pry this ball from its package and lay it on a new surface where the "poking" will begin. Here the Slimer will prod the slime with two or more fingers (with long, decorative nails), creating indentations and sucking sounds that Slimers call "thwocking." She doubles the slime over whenever it gets thin and begins the thwocking again. At twenty seconds, the slime is getting denser and she might take it into her hands and stretch it for the camera—though never past the frame of the viewfinder. Then, in one swift motion that all good Slimers know, she'll whip it around the back of her hand and wind the slime into a shape like soft serve. Otherwise she'll leave it on the table and do the whip right there. Then we know what's coming; she wraps both hands around the slime and squeezes until it seeps between her knuckles, popping and sizzling. Then she starts all over; the video runs on an infinite loop.

In 2012, I was being paid to read science fiction, employed as a TA for a Sci-Fi Lit class in a desert city whose mascot was a green Martian floating beside a greener cactus. . "We out here," the T-shirts said. For that job I wrote trick quiz questions, graded tall stacks of papers, and gave assigned lectures to students who were two years my junior. One of my first lectures was on a 1967 short story called "I Have No Mouth and I Must Scream," a story built simply of increasingly gruesome descriptions. The last five surviving humans are suffering psychological torture at the hands of a disembodied artificial intelligence known only as "AI." In the final scene, after the human protagonist has succeeded in mercy-killing his companions, AI turns him into a conscious ball of slime for eternity. Afterwards, the character thinks to himself, "I have no mouth and I must scream."

In 1994 my long-term babysitter Jessica, who lived across the street, began dating the actor David Coburn, the voice of Captain Planet, a cartoon figurehead of early '90s environmentalism who led the five Planeteers to battle villains like Verminous Skull, Duke Nukem, and Looey Gooey. Jessica brought my sister and a set of Planeteer rings—Earth, Wind, Fire, Water, Heart—so many that it was hard to play all the characters on our own. Just before she ended her romance with Captain Planet, she brought over the Captain Planet Toxic Sludge Dump: a doll-sized plastic doorway labeled "Toxico" that poured a bucket of green slop onto whatever action figure crossed its threshold. Even at that age, I understood that slime was accompanied by the sound of a sad trombone. Better than playing the villain, I liked getting to decide which Planeteer ring each player in the game should wear and at what time. Jessica, who had read my horoscope and my diary and told my parents what both contained, told me I was indecisive because I was born on a cusp between fire and earth signs. But I only cared that she let me wear one Planeteer ring on each hand so that we could start our game.

Some say the original Blob's slime was red to signal its parallels to the encroaching red scare, the fear of a different contagion. By the mid-90s, at Special Effects Unlimited, down the aisle from artificial blood, you could buy slime by the barrel, colored to order. There was slick black and toxic orange for oil spills, white for gory births like *Alien*'s, but green slime became a classic because it incarnated a certain fear. Historian Scott Poole argues that movie monsters do not, as previously believed, symbolize fears of the individual psyche. Instead, Poole suggests that new monsters are the incarnation of public anxieties specific to each successive era. In this thinking, as a contemporary society evolves, that society's monsters shift to signal new challenges rising to meet the status quo. Early vampires worked out their culture's fear of infectious diseases and homoeroticism in the same way, some argue, that vampires on TV and in movies in the early 1980s helped make the AIDS crisis a national concern. If so, what does slime prepare us for?

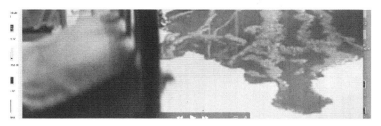

In 2018, the burnt river in Cleveland is the city's inside joke—a signal that the place can often feel like a drain sucking backwards towards some bleak, industrial past. I first flew into Cleveland above a sheen of brown and yellow that fanned out from the Cuyahoga river and marbled the lakefront like a plume. Sludge and oil. And for the first full year when friends who visited asked to see the lake, I could only get us fifty feet from water framed by chain link. My neighbors longingly reference the city's famous park system, "The Green Necklace," a string of green spaces that circle the water with old city blocks between. These same neighbors still laugh about the first time I requested directions to the parks, when I asked for a "pearl necklace" instead of the "Green."

Hughes, T. McKenney. Nature Magazine, 1910. "'In my

boyhood, I often lived on the coast of Pembrokeshire …
On the short, coarse grass of the hilly ground, I frequently
saw white, translucent jelly lying on the turf, as if it had
been dropped there … about as large as a man's fist.
Possibly there might be some pathological explanation
connecting it with sheep, large flocks of which grazed
the short herbage. But the shepherds and owners of the
sheep would have known if such an explanation were
admissible. They called it the rot of the stars.'" / "Other
welsh names are, or were, Chwyd awyr (literally, sky-vomit)
and Grifft ser (star-spawn) … but in the Penguin Dictionary
of British natural history, it is Pwdre ser or star-slime."
(*Handbook of Unusual Natural Phenomena*). / "The
evocation of sperm in such accounts is so obvious that
such finds were sometimes described as 'star shoot.' The
mythic relationship between the sky and the abject thus
has quite a long history" (*Aesthetics of Ufology*, 1982).

At my age, many of my friends are learning to tell the time
by inspecting what has landed in their underwear. Natural
Family Planning, "NFP," is the name of their method, as
described in *Our Bodies, Ourselves*. No condoms, no
pills, no children. Every morning, take your temperature.
Learn to recognize the remnants of ovulation, or

otherwise. "The information was always there," says my friend who practices, "I just had to start seeing." "What do you mean?" I ask her. "I had to stop seeing it as slime," she said, "but rather as something I could read."

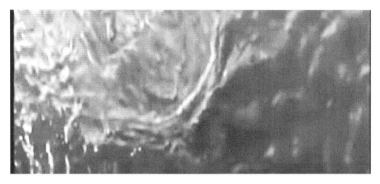

Early feminist critics read the money shot (or cum shot) as schadenfreude—the perverse pleasure that comes at the result of another person's humiliation. This included ejaculations onto the face, as well as onto another performer's body, such as the buttocks, chest, or mouth. The feminist critique extended to include arguments that the narratives delivered by current pornography were about the pleasure of "getting back at," "owning," or marking women "as used goods." More recently, in response, activists have urged that a reading of these acts is dependent on the reactions of those who receive a money shot. Scholar Lisa Moore suggests, more specifically, that male actors and other viewers are interested in evidence that their desire is reciprocated. Joseph Slade of Ohio University adds that, especially in the early stages of the porn industry during the '60s and '70s, when birth control methods were less reliable, the cum shot was a considerate, if not polite, gesture between actors.

QT m
QT m
QT m
QT m
QT m
QT m
QT m
QT m
Apple

My interest is in slimes on the move towards humans. In slime's role within narratives of pleasure and terror, though this curiosity stems less from experience than from continuous access to the internet. I was born after *Deep Throat* and *The Blob* made their waves, during the Nickelodeon age, and have only received one facial that was not dermatological. That experience is not of particular interest to me, though perhaps we will return later to the curious treatment of noun turned verb. Peter Sandor Gardos, film scholar, has argued that porn, like any document, must be read within its historical and social context: "Harm or degradation does not reside in the image itself." It was cameras and screens that instructed me how to arrange myself around others, not for my internal sensations, but to offer pleasure to other eyes and ears, to the eyes I had learned to imagine always upon me. Of note is that the cum shot does not require penetration. Cindy Patton, scholar/activist, situates the cum shot more broadly, as an element of the western sexual narrative. "No cum shot," she writes, "no narrative closure."

#slímconfession: Before all that, when we were twelve, my friend Tovah taught me how to orgasm. That night we'd stuffed ourselves into fake velvet party dresses and braided plastic chokers and unbuckled our shoes so we could run up and down the carpeted stairs in tightsfeet to work the coat check at my grandparents' Christmas party. Halfway through we snuck champagne into our Sprite and noticed that all of the coats were black and we hadn't used rack numbers. Later we soaked our feet, then our legs, then our hips in my grandmother's geriatric-style tub. Tovah demonstrated for me on her kneecap. "Like this," she said, pushing her wrinkled skin together with two fingers. I tried on my own knee, through the suds. "No, no," she said, "like this." The bath spilled over when we figured out we could hook our heels over the rim and lift our hips to face the air jets. Bini Adamczak: "What matters, of course, is never a question of what parts a body possesses, rather, of which parts of that body are put into action." And that's how it first happened, with my shoulder blades pressing against my best friend's back. Though I know this scene is strange and out of style for a generation who learns everything earlier, on a slender screen the length of their hand.

The Icelandic moss at the window carried a spider in with it. Or the moss tempted the spider to come in afterwards. Or a moss makes a good bed for anyone. One morning a spider is climbing there, king of the little hill, more likely its queen. What's true: either spiders are everywhere and not all of us notice them, or spiders follow me closely where I go. This time I have gone to Iceland. Three times I have ridden with spiders at my seat on an airplane. One time I found a spider dead in my braces. The Icelandic spider is drawn, as I am, to the window. I wake early and often, because of the light, and watch the dust motes as they drift slow from the ceiling. But this morning the motes are attaching to a web. The queen of the hill has built a perfect floor-to-ceiling net to catch me. Silver, to show the light between the bed and the door. Now she too will have to go outside. Above the roof of the barn there is a wind sweeping the cold from the glacier. Past the walls of the barn there is light and more light washing the hundred mosses and thousand turf clods that make it impossible to run without hooves. Beneath the floor of the barn is the placenta pit, a hole where the afterbirths of the sheep land once we press them through the floorboards to join manure that has rained there for a season. Beneath our feet, while we work, the pit works too, making a fertilizer that Ivan will spread across the fields come spring. By the third week, Ivan is sleeping off the night shift and plowing up the field, and it's just me and Birgitta in the barn.

Martin, the new farmhand from Croatia, has hands that don't fit inside a sheep, so he takes on other duties. By the fourth week, Martin, Birgitta, and I have given up all our shyness. We strip down to our underwear in the cold basement and hang our birth-damp work clothes, cargo pants and waffle shirts, on hooks where they'll stiffen and be crisp by morning. Nothing can be done about our parkas, all brown on one side. We pull on house clothes, scrub our arms with coarse brushes, and open the door to the first floor as steam fills the kitchen. Ivan is on the couch wearing a black tee-shirt that says "Fuck Google Ask Me" in an ancient-looking script. He'll be out in the barn again after dinner. Martin pulls a beer from the refrigerator and takes his first sip before the door closes. Katrina hands me a cold can—to share—because Birgitta is only thirteen. We fall into our seats at the table where Katrina's daughter Eydis drinks a Pepsi in all-black sweats, the family uniform, before going back to work at the hotel. At the other end, Viktor, eighteen, eats a pizza bagel on a glass plate with a coffee mug of milk, looks forward to a Rammestein concert in Reykjavik on Friday. We only see Viktor in the between hours because he sleeps all day and works in the barn alone at night, when he sometimes must go into the pit alone. Martin calls him "Sheepfucker" because the two of them are too close in height to get along, and also based on suspicions I'm not ready to hear more about.

The Dutch say slijm, and Germans use schleim, but it's slym in Africaans, and in Iceland they still use slím from the Old Norse. Further back there was the Latin limus (mud) and the Greek Limnē (marsh) to describe a material somewhere between water and earth. Limnitic land is land that floods or is contested. In the Bible, limnē refers to lakes, but mostly to lakes in hell, so that limnē most often describes a lake that is on fire. Slime's shared roots in Germanic, Italic, and Hellenic languages suggest something else deeply shared. But "slime" is somehow less and more than traditional onomatopoeia, less sonic than a moving word like "ooze." Perhaps "slime" more aptly mimics that close friend of sound, texture.

Language comes from the body, out of the mouth. But before language there is silence, there is a groan, a yell, a burble, a brush with grasses, a sucking in the mud. The shape of a landform does much to determine the shape of words. Here in Iceland, the isolation of island-living means that Ivan and his family can read Old Norse because modern Icelandic is so similar, so uninterrupted. The earliest people to arrive here (say some) were literate when they came, and so the island was first known by their material—Papir—the stuff of poor hermit monks who stowed themselves in the hills and read until Vikings arrived. My mother used to play an old song about a monk living in a cave by the sea with just a visiting bird to speak to. He was dying, I remember, from age or loneliness, or otherwise he drowned, though I'm not sure if these versions seemed very different to me then. The ancient Greek philosophers, and some modern linguists, maintain that the difference between the human and the animal is not sound making, but language, and that our ancestors developed language by mimicking natural sounds, so that most words began as onomatopoeia.

In the beginning, St. Augustine confessed to believing in Astrology. In the beginning, a farmer finds an unusual blob in his field and pokes it with a stick. The material quickly latches onto his hand and consumes him. It starts on the outskirts, where the farmer has been watching the sky and the fence line for generations, where the innocent shepherd sits beneath his tree, daydreaming and jerking off. In the beginning, there was the early soup of life that orbited oceans, biding its time, pooling in slick niches where it pulsed, throwing off the light, murmuring as it hugged the edges of coastline where the oldest of us would climb out. In the beginning, on an island in the arctic ocean, between the internet hour and sleep, between the bedroom window and the space where a spider tried to catch me, I'm reading books in one language about another, with my back against cold glass. I can't pronounce anything right, but I can smell my rank hair in any position. Rongorongo, the only script we know of that is native to the Pacific, is an island-formed language that has been lost to time and violence. An old name for Easter Island is Te Pito 'o te Henua, which means either "navel of" or "end of the world" because the island lies over a thousand miles from the nearest rock of land. One of the few surviving examples of Rongorongo is a crescent-shaped wooden ornament from the late nineteenth century with a line of carved glyphs that no living person can decipher, though not because Rongorongo wasn't written down, or tattooed on the backs of men, or carved into human skulls, and not because many haven't tried to read it since. Many examples of the writing that survived human history reveal that humans who could write and develop technology to preserve that writing believed they were living at the end of the world. Saints and monks, prophets and artists, astrologers and philosophers. Things had gotten out of hand, they thought. The world was changing fast, and the outcomes were impossible to conceive of. The process was surely building towards a culmination or release. And the moment before the climax is the best one, if we're being honest with ourselves. And if the climax weren't coming for us, that would mean we only fell somewhere near the middle. Soon, we would be dated, someone else's past. Flyover country. Dark age. So medieval monks who wrote about the second coming did it breathlessly. Those holy men were living what makers of the sci-fi thriller series *Black Mirror* have described about horror: that each of us imagines the apocalypse that will arrive in the form we deserve.

A "wet death" is the gory, splattery kind experienced in campy horror movies like *The Raft* and *The Blob*, named for the interior wetness of the blood released by objects that are wet before they kill. Critics of these genres often focus their analysis on who experiences a wet death, who creates it, and how the viewer reacts in turn. In comparative studies, several critics have drawn parallels between the ways that pornography and horror focus on the body and the similar reactions these genres prompt in an audience. Jay McRoy writes: "[Pornography and horror films] are both visceral. They both are about things happening to human bodies, [and about] having bodies on an intense sensorial level. Part of the point of those films—often precisely because they are exploitative—is to get the audience to react in the same visceral manner as [the bodies] depicted on screen."

ASMR (Auto Sensory Meridian Response), "The Unnamed Feeling," is a "low grade euphoria," attached to the sensation of static or "a mild electrical current," not unlike "the bubbles in a glass of champagne." Those who experience it say it begins as a tingling sensation on the scalp and moves down the neck and spine. I am reminded of Virginia Woolf, who described one character as being "like a mellow organ, but with a roughness in her voice like a grasshopper's, which rasped his spine deliciously and sent running up into his brain waves of sound." Many in the Instagram Slimer community use the hashtag #ASMR in their captions to collect audiences seeking out this particular experience.

There are hundreds of videos in the YouTube category "How to Take a Sliming," a genre the "Slimers" will tell you is different from their own. The videos depict classically beautiful cis-women getting doused in thick slime, though more are being deleted by the users themselves each day. The users in the videos, teenage to mid-twenties, from all over the world, mimic the choreography and the cadence of CinibelGómez1, who appears to be the genre's originator. CinibelGómez1 one year ago: "This was a very funny video I did custom for this channel. I enjoy it a lot, if you want personalized videos with more slime, many colors and now also foam in my face do not hesitate to write me cini********@gmail.com ♥." The spandex mini dress, the crossing and uncrossing, the bored expressions, the mention of going without underwear, the faceless man who turns the bucket in videos like "slimed in yoga pants," "Taking slime like a champ," or "The CORRECT way to take a sliming." In this genre, the mis-en-scène is close to a YouTube fashion tutorial or a prank, but the tone suggests fetish: "I can take a slime facial like the best of them," "This is bad but not as bad as a windy day going commando … How embarrassing that would be for me!" Often the videos are shot in the bathroom or otherwise outdoors, on a balcony, sometimes in a tub or the shower stall of a college dorm, wherever the slime can be contained.

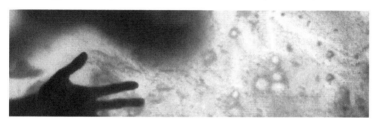

About the cum shot Linda Williams writes: "With this convention, viewers are asked to believe that the sexual performers [with vaginas] within the film want to shift from a tactile to a visual pleasure at the crucial moment of the male's orgasm … Nevertheless, it is always quite obvious that this spectacle is not really for her eyes." Among other things, Freud is famous for saying that everything tilts toward disorder, and that the orgasm is the closest a person can come to disorder and return unscathed. Shapelessness, the inarticulable. And a fear of death incarnated visibly by the loss and decay of familiar shape. Le petit mort, a glimpse of formlessness. The little death that moves us as close as we can get "to the thing that, once we touch, we can no longer report on."

Sleep
Paralysis.doc

One corner of the preteen Instagram Slimer community involves the topic of slime confessions or #slimeconfessions where, as caption to a new video, the Slimer will confess something small and ask others to reciprocate in their comments. The confessions aren't necessarily slime-related, but it's interesting to consider how the act of confession might stem from a quality specific to the kind of watching that slime videos invite—a solitary, receptive focus. The readiness for small hairs to stand on end. The ritual traditions of confession are often based in seeking the divine. #slimeconfessions increase the number of likes and comments and the number of times the video will appear on other followers' feeds. #slimeconfessions also function to invite personal investment from followers, and increase the feeling of community among watchers of a single or a select genre of slime sub-channels.

Mornings on the farm, I wake to a breeze under my bedroom door announcing Viktor and the smell of the night shift—cold grass at the front of him, sheep shit at the back. Nights, I fall asleep in sunlight, watching my fingertips finish de-pruning. This week, the flock is nervous and explosive because Martin is on spray duty. He climbs into a stiff jumpsuit and pulls his sweater up over his nose. Birgitta and I herd the fatties from their pens in batches, and by the time Martin has power-sprayed the floorboards clean of shit, the skin around his eyes has gone black and he's ornery. Afterwards, on placenta duty, Martin uses a pitch fork to lay a long organ across my lap and asks brightly, "Lunch?" Only he and Birgitta know I'm a vegetarian. He lifts our favorite black lamb out at arm's length and nods, "Perfect for a hotdog." Each new lamb is small and slippery. Sometimes a floorboard is jostled wide. Sometimes a hatch is left open by Martin or by Ivan. In the early season, when nights are dark, sometimes a lamb is crying out but nowhere to be found, down where the light makes gold pinstripes across the mire. Somewhere, there is a lamb sinking slowly. "Lambs drown," Birgitta told me, as if she has seen it. Above the couch where we are sitting, farmer Ivan has hung a spectrum of fox skins with skulls still attached. White, brown, ochre, grey, white. The Chihuahuas and I hate seeing them. The Arctic fox changes color with its landscape, Eydis says, and her father has collected five, one for each season, plus an extra white skin for the longest. Out the window beside the skins that hang like a mounted TV screen there's a spring snowstorm, rattling the house. I put my hand against the window and keep it there until the cold burns. Somewhere, the arctic fox is burrowing passages through deep snow. Ivan says that two summers ago, after the lambing finished, after the sheep were set to range free for the summer, it snowed ten inches in July. Miles from their farms, the flocks were stuck fast, snowed into the hills where they had been sleeping when the weather turned. From a distance, a search party on horseback spotted two flocks, grey against the white hillside, and sent up a cheer. The farmers rode in closer and the animals stayed quiet—some fragments— the foxes had eaten each sheep up from underneath and left their upper halves resting on the snow crust.

#slímconfession: In 1998, the year I turned ten, my grandparents took me to visit a remote island off of Norway, the place my grandfather's grandfather had fled potato famine for America just before The Great Migration. I remember that everything about Norway was white—the sidewalks, the seafoam, the tourists—that I was overdressed for the heat of the south, and that there were "nudie cuties" available in the magazine racks at every convenience store. Every evening, after the circuit of churches, Viking museums, and restaurants where my grandparents ate Lefse and pickled herring concurrently and so often they developed a combined odor I can't forget, they were ready for an early bedtime. Back in the hotel room, there were heavy curtains, pairs of red and blue slippers, and a tiny box television with cable and a single channel of softcore porn. The trick was that Norwegian adult programming had a seven-second preview wall, a setting that turned the screen pale green if a viewer didn't type in the proper permissions on her remote. My grandfather only spoke enough Norwegian to order coffee, attend church, and swear. But we figured out that if we flipped the channels quickly, back and forth, left-left-right-right, fast enough to avoid triggering the preview wall, we could watch a dirty pizza boy spliced with a soccer game and a news brief, all on local television— all fragments—pretending to each other that we were scrolling channels as grandma slept soundly.

Reports of inflamed jelly, Star-slough, star shot, star-fall'n are today thought to result from the discovery of gull vomit (the stork, reframed?), or nostoc—a kind of "short lived fungus"—or possibly the gelatinous remains of frogs and toads in the highlands. In literary terms, when a narrator discovers "inflamed gelly," "star-fall'n," or "star shot," the material serves as the illustration of disappointed hopes, "as when a man seeing a meteor fall, runs up and finds but a mass of putrid jelly." "Seek a fallen star and thou shalt only light on some foul jelly, which in shooting through the horizon, has assumed for a moment an appearance of splendor." -Walter Scott
"As he whose quicker eye doth trace

A false star shot to a mark't place

    Do's run apace,

And thinking to catch,

A jelly up do snatch."

  — John Suckling, 1541

"Flight distance" is the space a sheep will tolerate between itself and a perceived threat before it starts running away. Sheep have rectangular pupils, cannot feel well through their wool coats, do not defend territory or give chase. Sheep run. Sheep run due to *gregarious instinct* which compels them to follow the sheep in front, wherever it is going, to food or to slaughter, which is how four hundred

Turkish sheep once walked single file to their deaths in a ravine. Because of this, humans, especially the American individualist, often believe sheep are stupid. In a blog about slime monsters, one post describes the recurrence of "suicide by slime." This motif includes repeated instances in monster films like *The Blob* of a character ending their own life by diving from a height or flinging their body sideways into the path of the Blob, choosing slime as their narrative conclusion. "Flocking" is the reason there are sheep farmers, sheep dogs, lamb chops. Sheep follows sheep follows sheep follows sheep and soon the barn is moving across the pasture. As the flight distance dilates, as the flock moves away from a threat like a school of fish, the frightened animals on the outside of the flock press in towards the center, so that a flock on the move is folding on itself in a continuous loop while it is also traveling forward across space. The original *Blob* (1958) was produced by Valley Forge films, a Christian studio, as an attempt to regain financial stability. Sequels include *Son of the Blob* and *Beware! The Blob*, both in 1972. In the final scene of the 1988 remake of The Blob, a minister preaches to a crowd about the end of days. Before it was *The Blob*, the filmmakers considered titles like *The Glob*, *The Mass*, and *The Molten Meteor*. In *The Blob*, footage of the slime monster was created using a weather balloon, and later with colored silicone gel. The original Blob, a mixture of red dye and silicone, has never dried out and is still kept in the original five-gallon pail in which it was shipped to the production company, in 1958, from Union Carbide. After the Blob consumes its first victim, a doctor in the original film tells his nurse to dump some "trichloroacetic acid" on it, the stuff used to treat genital warts. The heroes eventually discover that cold temperatures are the Blob's kryptonite, and the monster is ultimately vanquished by a group of teenagers wielding fire extinguishers who manage to freeze it. The film ends after the US Air Force airlifts the frozen Blob to the arctic. The main character, Dave, explains, "while The Blob is not dead, at least it has been stopped." His father, Steve, replies, "Yeah, as long as the Arctic stays cold." "The End" title card appears on screen and then morphs into a question mark.

Before ASMR was coined, an alternative suggestion was "auditory induced head orgasm," but those active in online chatrooms and others in "the whispering community" objected to the term, resulting in a division in the ASMR community over the implication of mild sexual arousal. Afterwards, some videos were categorized as ASMRotica instead ("For obviously nothing could be more conventional than a money shot...," writes Williams, "it is a rhetorical figure that permits the genre to speak in a certain way about sex."). It's been estimated that Karin Garcia, the internet's "slime queen," makes between $80,000 and $160,000 a month through a full-time career making videos for the seven-million subscribers to her YouTube channel. Her videos draw preteens from the

Instagram Slimer community, but also exist on Youtube, the platform where "How to take a sliming" thrives. Most slime videos don't offer explicit narratives, feature dialogue, or characters. This is especially true for the ASMR slime genre made almost exclusively by the young, white femmes called "Slimers," who exist in the soft gap between ASMR and ASMRotica. Their most popular videos rack up hundreds of thousands of views. A large percentage of "Slimers" and their audiences from both camps use the word "satisfying" to describe this content, as in the slime compilation "TRY NOT TO GET SATISFIED," which has eleven-million views. Often, in their captions, popular Slimers will include anecdotes from their daily lives, detailed descriptions of the slime materials, confessions, or random musings that offer a personal context to the hands-only choreography in the video. Erotics aside, the sympathetic magic Slimers enact matches the often faceless and sonic landscape of mainstream porn, along with the implication that what is pleasurable for us to see and hear is pleasurable for the performer to feel. Elsewhere, "Slime Fest" is an outdoor concert series for families put on by Nickelodeon each summer, and "Slime Wave" is the name of a documentary on the movements of snails around a traditional British garden. But "Slime Fest" is also the name of a porn subgenre, and "Slime Wave" is also the name of an adult film series, versions 1-6. A quick search of appropriate databases reveals titles in the same genre: "Mud Bunny Chocolate Slime," "Two Lesbians Covered In White Slime," "Girls enjoy nice fucking in green slime," "Fist Full Of Slime Pussy Full Of Fist 2!!!".

Across the barn and shoulder-deep in a fat sheep crying out, Birgitta winces. She has perfect hands, but I'm the strongest. Even the loudest heavy-bellied sheep will run for it the moment any farmhand begins climbing into her pen. When the ewe finds a corner, I'll grab a horn in the quick manner Ivan showed me and press my right knee into her pillowy flank to pin her against the wall. From there, even a person with my wingspan can reach out and feel around in the wetness beneath her tail for the second pair of horns coming to light. It's the tiny muzzle that peeks out first with a little blue tongue as its flag. Sometimes a big boy will get stuck that way if his horns are more than an inch. When this happens, Birgitta and I have to poke one index finger from each hand inside— stretch the vulva wide the way a child stretches his cheeks out in jest. The sheep moans, and slowly the lamb's tongue gives way to shoulders. The point is to make sure it's the head before pulling. The point is to get the lamb out before the labor wave comes so fast that the new mothers are chewing at parts of their hot placentas while those still expecting nibble at tendrils left hanging out the backs of their friends. Ancient Greek and Roman medical theorists believed that women had two mouths— an upper and a lower—and treated maladies of the uterus by sending medicine down both necks, accordingly. In the second century AD, the authors of *Physiologus* wrote that the weasel receives semen by the mouth and so becomes pregnant. John Cleland's 1740 novel *Memoirs of a Woman of Pleasure* (known as *Fanny Hill*), generally considered the first pornographic novel in English, is Cleland's first-person account of Fanny, "an unpracticed simpleton who was perfectly new to life," who narrates her self-education as a 15-year-old sex worker. Early on, Fanny escapes an attempted rape when she gets a nosebleed (at the time, widely understood as blocked menstrual blood escaping through the face, and menstrual blood caustic enough to "excoriate [pull the skin off] the parts of men"). Written in an era when bleeding associated with "defloration" (loss of virginity) was highly eroticized and unbled girls were objects of extreme fetish, the rest of *Fanny Hill* is built of scenes depicting increasing amounts of "virgin gore" that spurts and flows ecstatically from "lesser necks." Medusa, for example, gives birth through her neck. Some of this helps explain why, in an article about the seminal vesicle, NetDoctor describes the gland's function as "caus[ing] semen to clot (become sticky or jelly-like)," "thought useful in reproduction for keeping the semen at the neck of a womb." Lips-mouth-neck-belly-neck-mouth-lips. All beginnings, no end in sight.

#slímconfession: I didn't watch *Texas Chainsaw Massacre* until the year I turned thirty, when I went to a punk show in Cleveland, full of thirty-somethings wearing black, where the film was projected on the wall of the warehouse behind the bassist. The drummer was scream-singing, using the proper breathing techniques, but his words got blurred against all the concrete. This went on for forty minutes—a good show. But in the moments after the music synced exactly with the pace of the rape-killing scene, I walked straight out the back door. The screaming had lost its irony, and I had suddenly stopped breathing. Here, perhaps as usual, I find myself confessing a lack of pop exposure. I have not seen enough horror to watch *gore* and think *slapstick* or *camp* (Throat, Dentata). Instead I write toward what I'm afraid of—perhaps a different way to see it—or perhaps toward something just past that gore that I have wanted to see all along.

Jay McRoy writes, "[In horror], like works of hard-core pornographic cinema, plot is pretense, an excuse for an intensive focus on the body's very materiality that, though an aesthetic informed by fragmentation and violence (both physical and semiotic), produces affect. As a result, it should come as no surprise that the camera work and editing techniques adopted by the directors of some of the genre's most notorious offerings bears a striking resemblance to those found in pornographic cinema." Of the money shot's first and most famous appearance, Linda Williams writes, "What was memorable in *Deep Throat* was precisely what most people disparaged about it: its 'threadbare,' 'poor excuse' for a plot. Yet in concentrating on this defect vis-à-vis other forms of narrative, critics missed the more important fact that …. For the first time in hard-core cinematic pornography, a feature-length film … managed to integrate a variety of sexual numbers." Linda Williams' aim in assessing the cum shot, which she calls "this most prevalent device of the new hard-core film's attempt to capture an involuntary confession of pleasure," is part of a much larger project to understand hard-core pornography through the ways that it "speaks."

When the Spaniards landed on Easter Island in 1722, they handed indigenous chiefs a document claiming the land in the name of their king, and the Rapanui signed in their own manner, with drawings of frigate birds and vulvas. By

1871, about ninety-four percent of the population had been enslaved or killed by new illnesses. But in 1886, Ure Va'e Iko, a Rapanui steward of the last chief, was forced to "read" one of the last remaining tablets containing Rongorongo for an American naval officer who was visiting, though he likely recited an old song instead, out of fear. One of the lines he delivered was a "procreation chant," a series of paradoxes: "Itchiness copulated with Badness: There issued forth the kape taro"; "The fish Rat-Tail copulated with Maggoty Hina: There issued forth the whale"; "Parental God copulated with the Slimy Vagina of God: There issued forth the deep sea." The invisible flood, the waters that subsume. The "invisible orgasm" is pleasure without evidence—blood, slime, penetration—blooming "in the wonders of the unseen world." Williams' argument is ultimately about the money shot as part of a narrative that "is constantly soliciting and trying to find a visual equivalent for the invisible moments of clitoral orgasm." Though perhaps what is most visible is the confirmation of formlessness as also a means to "top."

Science is interested in spider silk in large quantities for artificial human ligaments, for bulletproof vests and airbags, but whenever they try to set up spider farms, the spiders kill each other because webs are, in the most basic sense, territory. In July of 1973, after some prompting, Arabella spun a complete web in zero gravity while orbiting the earth inside a box shaped like a window frame. Her friend, Anita, built none. Arabella ate her first web aboard Skylab, as spiders sometimes do, to save energy, and then built a second, more elaborate version, much finer than webs found on earth. She died of dehydration. Other than the ability to spin silk, the Spider Goats born at the University of Wyoming were like any other goats. They brayed and leapt and called for their mothers. Researchers harvested the silk they spun from their nipples to build materials with nanofibers, nanomeshes and BioSteel, all things you could buy for a while on the world wide web, sometimes called "the net."

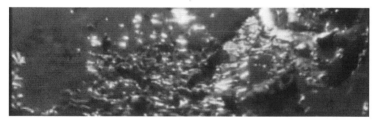

ChatRoulette was invented by a seventeen-year-old Russian coder who learned about "Russian Roulette" by watching American movies. The active website pairs webcams at random and allows users to type messages once they are paired. In 2010, ChatRoulette had 35,000 visitors a day, and one study found that users were more likely to find an unmanned webcam than one featuring "a woman alone." The same study found that a user was more than twice as likely to encounter a handwritten sign requesting "female nudity" than to encounter a femme in the nude.

The queen of the moss hill had to leave. She had tried to string me up, wring me out. She was starving in unfriendly territory. Perhaps she could smell the blood I had not washed from my skin entirely and the blood beneath it always washing. A spider web is made of proteinaceous silk, the kind I had to pull down to leave the tank of light, the kind that is only protein, the kind healers first stuffed inside human bodies to staunch wounds and what poured from them. There is "sticky" spider silk and "fluffy" spider silk for capture, spider silk for traps and for houses, sheets and baskets, cones and orbs. And some spiders do weave and cast their own nets, like Spiderman. To be "black widowed" is a term that names a domination narrative and describes a power dynamic implicit in porn that suggests perhaps, after sex, a dominating femme will eat her partner. Footage of doms and subs in bondage, centered in decorative webs, accompany. And perhaps this mainstream hetero-staging, like all others, blooms from a concern that the one who is penetrated has always been more "powerful" because their pleasure is "unseen." Maybe it is faked or maybe it is larger. Splooge quantifies, jizz measures, but maybe pleasures kept invisible have workings that are hidden beneath the floorboards for good reason. Cum is a shame by contrast, a confession made material, vulnerable. Spiderman, worked up. So I position my body to receive the lens.

It's sixty degrees in the afternoon in the last weeks of lambing season, and the barn is emptying out. Ivan has chased every mother outside with her twins or triplets into the acreage where they can eat grass, huddle against the gale, and fertilize fields where the hay is gathering its strength. The old sheep stands on her own, swiveling her ears like satellite dishes. She knows the voices of her lambs individually. Out there, she'll kick at any old lamb nosing around for its mother and call out names when her twins roam too far. Tensions inside the barn are dispersing as the crowd thins, and on some cold, bright evenings, the empty pens become a basketball court where Martin, Eydis, Birgitta, and I shoot hoops in our parkas and work boots. The game is horse, or "Asna" (Ass), slow enough that most of it is spent standing and drinking, checking in occasionally on the sheep. Whenever we dribble, the ball makes a slap from the times it has rolled away and gone slick in all the placentas I haven't forked up today. Eydis and Birgitta tell me that afterbirth is good for the skin. Eventually, Eydis pulls my beer from my hand. "Go help the screaming one," she says impatiently, giving orders like her mother in the kitchen. I have to pause and close my eyes against the familiar din of moans and bleats to pick out the urgent pitches of a scream that Eydis started hearing five minutes ago. I extricate the purple lamb.

When "Asna" ends, the four of us walk together up to the farmhouse, late for dinner, a little drunk. Katrina leaves the potato soup on the stove and sits us down for a meeting. Her daughter holds back a knowing smirk. "Someone has used up all the internet. I am not pay for more gigs," says Katrina, scanning the crowd, each with a smartphone in their hand or pocket. The pot gently boils over. Birgitta and I flick eyes at each other. "Someone will explain me," says Katrina, "what is 'you-jizz.' What is 'chat-roulette'?" But Katrina pronounces it "you-yizz," and I snort into my beer at the far end of the table. She glares at me for a long moment. From this angle, only I can see a pink flare climbing the side of Martin's neck.

#slímconfession: My college boyfriend clicked "spin" and set his hands on my shoulders to bend me forward, carefully, keeping our faces out of the webcam's reach. The website's preview window reflected two pale bodies on a white comforter, a set of dusty blinds. He moved inside me when the first round landed us on an unmanned camera and, with his left hand, he clicked "Spin" again, rocking against me with his chin kept high. "Spin." A man's chest. "Spin." A man's chest. "Spin." A group of teenagers. A man masturbating. "Spin." A face and a grey beard. "Alright!" our match typed immediately and then, "she's hot," which made my boyfriend pause and me flush for the moment it took the man to write "now put it in her ass." With his left hand, my boyfriend typed the keystroke for "thumbs up" and then hit "Spin" so that we moved perpetually forward and across the world, ever more briefly. He eventually came on my back, as always, for a Korean man wearing a top hat, and for a moment afterwards the three of us waited on camera, out of breath, as the material pooled in the hollow of my sacrum.

When it's all over in "How to Take a Sliming" videos, the performers seem unsure about what to do next—part the curtain of slime falling over their mouth? Windshield-wipe their eyes? Remember to smile. Most videos end quickly as the performers squeegee their faces with their hands. They know we have what we came for, and for them the cleanup has only just begun. Some of the performers conclude by talking through the slime, by asking the audience what they'd like to see in the future—what kind of slime next time and how much? What should I wear? And the viewers respond in kind: "Pour slime in your high heels and walk around so we hear the squelch in your toes." "Two buckets of green slime, a bucket of red again and again without stopping in a bikini." "Take off your underwear and rub it in the slime." In a different arena, some of the slime videos in the regular Instagram ASMR genre expand to include users with delicate, decorative nails cutting soap, whispering, and crinkling paper. One specific user wears long, white bell sleeves in all of her videos and often comments about how close her sleeves came to touching the sticky slime she "thwocks" in each iteration. The satisfaction of getting all the batter out of the bowl with a spatula. Of excavating a tough booger from your nose. A rice crispy treat, stretched. The hands cannot move out of focus. The camera cannot sit on the table. The torso can never appear. The pokes can't be too slow. The slime can't be off-center. A video on "Pet Peeves About Slimers" concludes with, "When the slime rips, oh my lord." The loop should be maintained—the slime should never, ever, tear.

About movie slime, Mike Kelly writes, "The horrific nature of many blob monsters stems from their thinly veiled genital appearance, it is only a short step, as a viewer, to strip this veil away to embrace them as overtly erotic images. Not to do so would be to buy into the repressive sexual attitudes of those that would depict the genitals as monstrous and alien ..." Linda Williams writes that, though the cum shot appeared in early porn films as a new narrative element that shifted the structure of the genre: "It was not until the early seventies, with the rise of the hard-core feature, that the money shot assumed the narrative function of signaling the climax of a genital event .... Previously, hard-core sequences tended to be organized as discontinuous, relatively nonlinear moments of genital show in meat shots offering visual evidence of penetration. Each shot—'meat' or 'money'—is emblematic of the different 'climax' of its generic form."

#slímconfession: I met my best friend Clairetta on a bathroom floor in Junior High. She saw me first, after I sat down beneath the hand dryer. Clairetta had her back against the block-concrete, her face a deep red around the eyes like mine. We looked at each other and put our heads against the tile, said something about *dying*. No one had told us about sixth grade club basketball or the workouts other girls had been doing that summer before seventh grade began. We dropped out of basketball and were friends going forward. Slept separately with the same men. After college, after Clairetta came out to me and to her siblings, we met at a new bar near my parents' house in Iowa, raising our eyebrows about the polished steel and the tufted, fake-leather booths. Clairetta leaned between our drinks and drew me two line graphs on a pair of beverage napkins. Tension ascended the X axes, and time moved along the Y. The first graph described heteronormative sex, and the second represented the queer kind. When she leaned away, I recognized in her first graph the leaning peak of dramatic structure—Set-up, rising action, climax, and the sharp drop of dénouement that she had labeled "(sleep)." Beside this, the second graph escalated quickly. It flat-lined high up, fell midway, lifted slightly into a second and third reveal, then pitched low and turned itself into a knot labeled "hand-holding and snacks." The line rose again and turned into a waveform labeled "time traveling," reached a fourth peak and fell, near the edge of the napkin, towards a conclusion called "distractions."

For a book rabidly obsessed with "first times" and bloody scenes of "defloration," of note is that critics rarely mention that *Fanny Hill* [1740] opens with Fanny's account of her body ecstatic for the first time in the arms of Phoebe, an older sex worker who is enlisted to initiate the girl: "Every part of me was open and exposed to the licentious courses of her hands, which, like a lambent fire, ran over my whole body, and thaw'd all coldness as they went." Later in *Fanny Hill*, as in 18th century London, Fanny and other young sex workers are able to re-stage and re-sell their own virginities again and again by using complex props such as a "little fish bladder of blood" inserted just before sex, or a bottle of "red stain" kept in the bedpost, to serve customers what they pay for; an "economy of fluids." Mid-way through the novel, when Fanny is deflowering her lover's male servant ("a blushing simpleton"), Fanny herself bleeds profusely, for real, marking the moment of his defloration and rendering the consummation of his pleasure visible in her own body. As in all such images of the era, we are to understand, as Howard Bloch describes, that "there can be no difference between the state of desiring and of being desired." Because such scenes—and their re-making of corporeal events believed to be singular—allow Fanny's story to be "primarily arranged around this thematic trope" (and the paradox of infinite virgin gore), early critics like Antje Schaum Anderson and Tassie Gwilliam read the structure of *Fanny Hill* as one that "serves to disrupt the traditional linear sexual initiation plot." But even Cleland can't resist closure, and at the very end a contrite Fanny, bored of her exploits (and the fears of a "real maid" replaced with "those perhaps greater, of a disassembled one") marries the man who "first purchased her maidenhead." Harvard child psychiatrist Steven Schlozman says that in both literature and among his current patients, he has noticed a tendency to romanticize end times—the version of an Armageddon a person believes they will survive. And so perhaps what appeals to us about the Blob is what appeals to us about a neat conclusion—justice served. *Perry Rhodan*, the weekly German Sci-Fi Pulp Magazine that has run continuously since 1961, has featured every type of slime, including "The Willies," who are feminized, emotional blob monsters who provide comic relief when they panic at anything that goes wrong, as well as evil slime monsters that cover the entire planet in a layer of slime (Sherwin Williams, based in Cleveland). In *The Thing* (1982), a group of American researchers living in a station in Antarctica encounter a formless creature that crash-landed there in 100,000 BC. The audience never sees The Thing's original form, because it exists by inhabiting other hosts. What is terrible about The Thing is not only that it possesses bodies, not that it could be any of us, but that it is, by nature, formless. But there is often something primal, more ancient than textural, about the fear of a slime monster. Something we forgot to tell our children. Slime is terrifying because it is alive, but shows no signs of animal structure. Not two mouths but all receiving. All Mouth, all the time. In western culture, of course, one of our earliest versions of apocalypse takes the form of an endless and all-consuming flood.

Philip Brophy writes that horror "tends to play not so much on the broad fear of Death, but more precisely on the fear of one's own body, of how one controls and relates to it." As many critics of "movie monsters" have established, a fear of slime, like a fear of the vampire, feeds into a conception of "otherness." But what slime incarnates today, more particularly, is the fear of disintegrating boundaries—the dissolution of borders that pen dualism and basic resources in with cults of individualism. A slime monster is easy for a mainstream audience to fear, but that fear becomes difficult to name because it incarnates the presence of specters like Global Warming, the AIDS virus, and the Great Pacific Garbage Patch, all of which audience members recognize but many of which they still feel distant from. McCroy adds that "horror films often create fear by exploiting the all-too-human trepidation over the potential loss of physiological integrity, a dread that manifests itself through the spectator's body as it squirms and writhes in its seat, assuming the terrified postures akin to those projected upon the screen." Slime is different from the vampire because it is a material being we can't quite see or imagine, but which might contain us whole and force us to participate. Slime is different because when slime eats a person, when it pushes out the back of their eyes, that person dissolves into a different body and becomes collectively implicated, not a new monster but part of the devouring whole.

One week until the end of the season now, and we can't keep up with all the births. Eydis and Ivan have joined us and even Martin is trying to help. Things get bad when a lamb gets stuck or suffocates inside the placenta or when the lamb's mother lays on it or goes on chewing her hay. Things get bad when I find a shiny purple sac alone in the corner and tear open the bag with my fingernails, press up-down-up on the wet, blue lamb. When I'm lucky, it flops like a caught fish, coughs twice, breathes air. The Icelandic word for lamb is "lamb," and this morning Birgitta and I pull another dead one from its mother. Birgitta rises, walks over to the warming pen, and lifts the smallest motherless one into her arms. She stands the new lamb up on four legs, holds the dead one by the neck, and rubs the stillbirth's smell all over. The orphan lamb cries as loose hooves clock its head. Life and death play tag in the corner. My little teacher stretches the placenta out like a fresh lavender coat, and the live one shimmers as she nudges it toward mother.

You've likely heard of Harry Harlow who, in 1950, ran a

study on the role of physical contact between mother and child in primates (rhesus monkeys) involving inanimate surrogate mothers. To conduct his experiment, Harlow built two mother figures, one built of wire that held a bottle with food, and a second made of cloth that held no food at all. In each trial, the baby rhesus visited the wire mother to eat and rushed back to the cloth version, where it clung. Some of the scarier studies getting air time this year reveal that the number one predictor for early mortality, above smoking, above lack of exercise, obesity, and high cholesterol, is social isolation. Screen time allows for participation in a community from anywhere, at any time. But what it prevents is physical contact. It seems to me, here on the farm, that our obsession with digital slime is less about community and more about our collective and expanding isolation, our distance from intimacy in the form of texture and touch.

In pornography, the term "money shot" came from earlier film projects as a term to describe a moment of climax that cost the most dollars to film in terms of special effects. Later it came to mean the shot that *made* the most money. Consequently, in porn (though the logic is long to string), actors with penises were paid more per shot. On Nickelodeon, green slime machines were also making money shots on a channel that grew in popularity after it incorporated slime. In lambing terms, slime also announces the most lucrative moment in a sheep's life, prior to slaughter. In October 2017, the underwear thief Jonathan Ruiz was finally apprehended in California after breaking into a house where four college girls were living. He had strewn their underwear about, used a laptop to masturbate, ate several cookies from the refrigerator then left a carton of milk on the counter and traces of his semen on a keyboard, which is exactly how he was caught.

#slímconfession: The first time I touched a sheep, I touched a book. If you study books, the oldest kind, sewn and scraped and written with hands, the keepers will encourage you not to use gloves. Because the oils from your hands and the oils from hands of other readers plucking for a thousand years at the edges of these pages, which by now have grown dark and full of digit oil, have helped to preserve that book, which is itself made of skin. A book made of skin is a thing of horror (*Hocus Pocus*), but most books were once sheep or cows. Books that were sheep were called parchment. On surviving pages, a reader can still find DNA from the noses of certain priests who kissed books a thousand years ago. On some of these pages there are holes that stretched open after the skin was scraped of hair and flesh. Holes from the skin of a real sheep, once hidden below a woolen coat, where sheep have moles and scars, and books might too, if monks didn't cut them out. Sometimes savvier monks used those holes in the design of their pages. Some monks repurposed them as peep-holes to upcoming, significant words, and others embroidered the holes shut, as in one manuscript where the monk-artist has fashioned a hole into the design of a spider's web, thought by some experts to be a reference to a Bible verse, and by others to the folk belief that the alphabet began when a human used his finger to trace the shapes made by a spider's silk. A storyteller is often named Arachne. But a sheep is more than pages. The sheepskin was stretched for parchment, the mutton was cooked for a meal, the sheep's bones were charred and ground for pigment, and sometimes, unbeknownst to the monks, or maybe not so (monks were farmers), the sheep intestines were cleaned and tied off and sold or gifted as condoms.

In an article on the history of Rongorongo, the language native to Easter Island, critic Jacob Mikanowski writes that "Undeciphered scripts work like Rorchach blots. Lacking a defined meaning, their inscrutability allows their would-be interpreters to project their fantasies, wishes, and desires onto the blank space they hope to fill in." Dr. Allen Carroll, a Sydney physician, and the father of "rongorongo fringe," tried his hand at a translation of the script carved into the wooden artifact: *To those who are our Guardians, oh give ear to us in your temple. You are our protectors … Ye gods.* Henryka Romanska, a Polish folklorist, did too: *"The bird gladly with the flower flies / The bird gladly with the fruit flies."* The most sustained effort by linguistics scholars in St. Petersburg led to Irina Fedorova's attempt, in which one Rongorongo text concludes: *"yam, yam, taro, taro, he cut a tuber of yam, he took a tuber of taro, a tuber, a tuber, he dug up, he cut, he cut, taro, turi sugar-cane."* Mikanowski points out that this translation comes closest to the Rongorongo oral tradition, which was most often sung, and often expressed "the surprise of being alive and also the sadness of life." "May it forever remain a riddle we can't parse," writes Mikanowski, "a joke whose punchline is forever slipping from our grasp." The end is often the beginning—one joke signals another. And pornography is not the culprit of anything, but only a cultural material. My interest in porn is in porn as context—what we can read in slime about ourselves through its tropes and scaffolding. Critic Jay McRoy has described pornography as a genre structured through a series of close-ups, or "meat shots," depicting "graphic intersections between genitalia and other bodily zones …

coded as erogenous." In the same study, McRoy has read horror films "As texts designed around excessively gory displays of the human form ripped open or disintegrated, splatter films frequently rely upon special effects rather than tightly constructed—or even remotely logical— narratives to produce an impact on their audience." Williams reminds us that during *Deep Throat*'s first reveal, when the character Linda learns the oral technique from her doctor that brings him to orgasm, the money shot is "narratively presented as simultaneous with Linda's own long awaited climax— that is enhanced by intercutting with fireworks, ringing bells, bursting bombs, and firing missile."

"Ivan's got the shotgun," says Martin, breathless. "He's shooting Old Sheep. Want to watch?" I say nothing but follow Martin into the field where Ivan has one foot on the old sheep's neck. This is the name we use for her— the grey one, balding, satellite ears—the one who can't nurse anymore. And how many lambs in her lifetime? She's stopped moving entirely. Ivan gently pushes the barrel against her temple. He fires one shot and her body goes stiller than before. I never visited the placenta pit, but I did think about the darkness rising wetly beneath that barn, a gaping mouth. Its floorboards, jostled teeth. The pit swallowing lambs and the placentas they rode in on, the muck spreading darkly across the fields, the hay there growing into young chutes, gorged and digested by sheep, injected into ewes, ripening and swelling and falling, slipping, again through the floorboards of the barn. Two days left on the farm, and soon I will ride the hot bus south, to the library. Back in the yellow apartment, I will wake each morning, zip on a half-brown parka, and study documents close to the harbor. There I will be a researcher. There, I'll be sure of the facts. The wind is low and I will not half-sleep with the lights on. I will not dream that the front door is opening, opening. The sun will go down, and I will not dress hastily in the windowless bathroom, will not be haunted by the ghost of the landlord's mother (she likes when I keep the place clean). I will touch other bodies. I will not watch footage of preteen hands looping, crushing, stretching, thwocking late into the night. Will not post pictures of pretty lambs that later died. The smell will come out of my clothing. I will obey the rules of the laundry. I will not bring home the large underpants of other ladies. Or try to return them, hours later, to the drying line among garments seemingly also theirs. I will find where the dumpster is located. The night will be black, the days will get shorter, and my only friends will not be the Iraqi gas station attendant, the lady at the yarn shop who yells at me with her hands, the book cart with the squeaky wheels and the green felt shelves, the handwriting of the poet who drew the zodiac inside his "O" in 1923, the spider that comes in with the wildflowers, the vase that becomes her landscape, the ooze that grows at the bottom, the mess on the balcony after leaving her out all night to get some air.

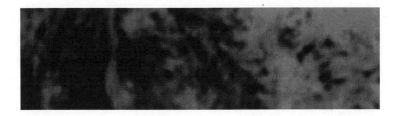

In 1970, five art handlers from MoMA wearing full-body suits mixed the original 8,000 pounds of bentonite and water used in "Mud Muse." They poured cartons of the powdered, clay-like bentonite into twenty-gallon buckets and mixed their batches with the type of industrial-sized immersion blenders used in construction. The finished mud bubbled in time with the music playing beside it through a complex network of air pumps that could sense sound. It was one of the earliest pieces that featured digital material influencing the motion of physical matter as art, what a MoMA curator called "an emerging sign of our own digital age." Because of Karin Garcia and content creators like her, Elmer's glue sales rose twenty-five percent in 2016. The original recipes for YouTube and Instagram slime included a mixture of Elmer's glue, borax, and water. Hip primary school teachers now use slime recipes to teach students about everything from Ocean Cleanups to Gravity. Now that borax fear has spread among mothers, you can skip the chemical and use glue, contact lens solution, shaving cream, and baking soda. Add beads or aquarium pebbles for crunchy slime. Kinetic sand for sinking sand slime. More shaving cream and glitter for Fluffy Unicorn slime. Shift the ratios for the Galaxy, Iceberg, Metallic, Green Monster, Chocolate, and Tacky versions, or enough Cloud Slime to fill a bathtub. In some cases, witnesses in the 20th century reported finding piles of "star shoot" large enough to fill a wheelbarrow, which would rule out the involvement of a single animal. There are all kinds of other theories about star slime: the gel from diapers thrown out of jumbo jets, or the gel used to seed hurricanes. The most common characteristic of "star shoot" is a rotten smell, and also that it evaporates very rapidly, removing all physical evidence in a matter of minutes. "Here, we shall allow the problem to rest for the time-being. If in the future anyone should discover gelatinous substances 'in the field' or, as in the Cambridge event of 23 June 1978, to witness such matter gliding down through the air, we should appreciate receiving a sealed bottle of it for further research and examination."

slime

In the end, when the Blob arrives, will it smell like Pine-Sol or Wintergreen? Or will it be unbearably rotten? Extinguish the local vultures as a bare bulb draws moths? Hot when it catches us, or cold and sudden like the darkness between rows of corn? It's a particular fear that a sticky green inspires. Slime, the digester, suspender, time-eater, slow-seeper. The green of rot, of swamps, of snot, green apples, poison-frog green, cactus after rain, cartoon-fart green, fast-cash green, witch-nose green, thermonuclear green, bottom-of-the-lake green, the green of what predated the body and of what comes after. Because slime does have a shape—it is the shape of pouring, the shape of excess, of orifice, cycle, untied margin, broken plane. And gravity, slime's master, a kind of wanting. What slime also wants— to stay down, never severed or put out, to multiply, stick, become sac-like, form dew drops, spread or jiggle, collect itself, never be confused about its fodder. The horror of slime lies at the heart of other fears we've enumerated; that fear of whatever will someday move through us as men once moved through buffalo. Not a disease or top predator, but body giving way to body, earlobe to heel, mantle to crust. In Mike Kelly's close reading, "Sartre's analysis of the slimy most definitely addresses the sexually horrific overtones of such substances, whose clinging qualities he designates as... genitals, and in fact all holes, provoke in him the same fear of being swallowed up."

#slímconfession: I have never eaten mutton, but I have eaten a lamb. On our last weekend off in my first year of farming, my boyfriend and I traveled to a monastery by bus. We were bone-sore. Monasticism was fading. In the high-walled city, poor monks were renting vacant rooms to travelers with twenty euro and a passport. My boyfriend forgot his passport. Night was falling as I cried in a medieval alley with my backpack still strapped to my torso. Once I quieted I remembered the photocopies in the inner pocket. We bought a bottle of wine and knocked again at the door of the monk who gave us keys and pointed down a long, cold hallway. Each doorway had a portrait of a previous monk in residence frescoed above it, each gaze set so straight that it followed. As we crossed our threshold, I felt our own pious man roll his eyes backwards into our square chamber with its bureau and its wide, hard mattress. We drank our bottle in the room, standing up, and left our backpacks on the floor to find a table and a second bottle on the street. The lights of the small, rural city were blinking out as we uncorked a third, and back at the monastery we were out of breath when I pushed him up against the door. The eyes in the hallway rolled inside their frescos as we handled each other roughly, kneading at something we'd held back onthe farm. He put his fingers in my mouth and I tasted the dirt beneath his nails. It was the only time he tossed me hard against a wall. At the end, he straddled my chest, made the kind of eye contact that feels like speaking. I expected what was coming, but when it hit my chin I laughed abruptly and so did he. From the folds of his robes our monk presented a sad trombone. But in that moment a certain whirring inside me stopped, and a feeling I had been waiting for finally arrived.

Is a set of knuckles, is a palm, more intimate than a face? Is touching better than seeing? In a disembodied lineup, I can identify each person I've loved by their hands. It can hurt to stare too long at my mother's hands, or to see the hand of an old heartbreak in a social media stream, wrapped around a pint glass at the edge of the frame. In the morning, when I wake beside my lover in the dark, it will be their hand that I reach for. I use screens for work, for writing, for making art, for fixing lamps, for growing houseplants, for playing games, for keeping friendships, for fighting with my sister, for zoning out, for zooming in, for making-up, for taxes, for planning dinner, for watching eaglets hatch on a far mountaintop, for selling furniture I bought with exes, for buying baby shoes, for ordering pizza, for getting off. Through screens, mine has established itself as a visual culture. But what my visual media is gradually revealing is that I want all my images to approximate touch.

A rhizome, a grid of velvet ropes, an infinity room of desktop monitors, a net—we still struggle to represent the internet visually because we cannot touch it, yet it envelops us. Bini Adamczak: "Think of how a net catches fish, how gums envelop their food, how a nutcracker crunches nuts, or how a hand encircles a joystick, a bottle of beer... " The history of the internet is as much an inventory of knowledge, a mechanism of globalization, as it is a highway for viewing, displaying, and experiencing types of intimacy. A permissive space that exposes many users to the variety of fetishes preferred, confessed, and invented by humans looking into screens across the planet. Via visual and auditory platforms, inventive content-creators do what they can to touch us, to represent the kind of multiplicity that is deeply invisible but perhaps closest to the thing internet users seek out. "Gaze Theory," based on the language of "male gazing," is a theory of representation, not of looking or touching. Williams: "The conceit of *Deep Throat*: the placement of the clitoris in the [protagonist's] throat is a repositioning that aligns the [visible] orgasm with the face's power of expression." And looking long into the internet offers a sensation of being continuously on the brink, at the cusp of an answer, a connection, a release. Looking away, tearing our gaze from the screen, is a kind of apocalypse that pulls us back from that precipice. The first "gaze theory" was based on an alignment of sexuality and financial power that shaped formal composition. The cool customer sits in a cis-hetero easy chair. The image tells the customer he is right. Anderson: "On the contrary, I seek to expose the constructedness of plot and pleasure within a patriarchal, heterosexual economy of narrative and of erotics." And so rather than framing the first work of literary porn in English as an example of some kind of "feminine" plot, Anderson demonstrates that *Fanny Hill* is a narrative form that falls between the extreme tropes of "absence" and "excess" traditionally associated with those who are penetrated, and concludes that the novel's repetitive sequence "suspends linearity," creating a space where plot lines "cross gender boundaries as frequently and with as many consequences as narrators, readers, or characters do." Fanny Hill's father was a maker of nets. And the gaze I describe is not the linear motion of human looking into screen, but of the loop of gazing and representing that confirms a multiplicity of desires, that reorient seats of power again and again. The all-consuming gaze radiates from "feeds" aiming not into the lazering pupil, but into the yawn of the throat. Slime on camera—the infinite gaze returned.

This is the end. All but ten sheep have finished laboring. The pit needs airing. Martin has power-washed the barn floor twice. I've given different hugs to Ivan and his daughters, to Katrina and Martin, to Birgitta, then the sheepdogs and the newest crop of lambs who cry at the sight of my blue parka and clamber into my lap—Ivan has said no bottles today. Katrina drives me to the bus stop, and I take the hot coach south, riding on high roads towards the sea, the sky so full of light it seems to tilt away from us. When the red clock above the driver says 15:00, I know the flock is being thinned from the fields. The ewes are growing intolerably loud in the driveway as Ivan herds the lambs into the slow, high-walled truck, just in from town, keeping its engine running. Back in Reykjavìk I wash my hair three times in sulfuric water so hot it blisters my shoulders. I've been conspicuously absent for weeks, and Sven's wife has invited me to dinner every one of them. So I paint my nails to cover the stains and wear my last clean shirt to Sunday dinner. I was touched in a manner that made other touches hard to bear. By now Ivan is watching TV beneath a year of skins. Victor and Eydis are eating cereal at the table, tired but restless, out of their routine. Eydis says the ewes will cry for their lambs until they fall asleep. In the southern city, Sven's wife sits two blonde children on my lap and Sven posts the photo to his feed. I'm stiff all over, not clean enough, not my hands. His wife and daughters feed me cold cocktails and hot bread wet with herb butter all balanced on a plate over their white carpet. Milk eyes looking nowhere. They sit me unsteadily in the middle of a long oak table that is better dressed than I am. Out comes the main course, grey and steaming. The matriarch spreads a pool of mint jelly and she passes me the first cut.

List of Images

Figure 1: "The Blob." Irvin S. Yeaworth, director. *The Blob*. Tonylyn Productions, 1958. A black-and-white film still of a dark, shiny, viscous blob filling most of the video frame. Screenshot by the author.

Figure 2: "Girl Slimed in Bathtub." Video no longer available because the account has been terminated. A black-and-white video still of a person sitting on the edge of a bathtub with slime falling down the front of their torso. Screenshot by the author.

Figure 3: Instagram video from the user "poppingslim3." A black-and-white still of a right hand with manicured nails "poking" a pool of opaque slime. Screenshot by the author.

Figure 4: "The Green Slime." Kinji Fukasaku, director. *The Green Slime*.1968. A black-and-white film still featuring the hands and knees of an astronaut who is wearing a white space suit and bending to pick up a tool covered in green slime. Screenshot by the author.

Figure 5: "The Blob." Yeaworth, Irvin S., director. *The Blob*. Tonylyn Productions, 1958. A black-and-white film still of viscous material temporarily forming damp cylinders as it presses itself through the windows of a projection room into the seating area of a movie theatre with floral wallpaper. Screenshot by the author.

Figure 6: "Mud Muse (1968-71)." VernissageTV. A black-and-white video still from "Mud Muse" installed at the MOMA, featuring a close-up of a low, glass trough filled with thin, bubbling mud. Screenshot taken by the author.

Figure 7: "The Raft." From "Creepshow 2." 1987. Michael Gornick, director. A black-and-white film still featuring rippling, dense material floating on the surface of a lake from birds-eye-view. Screenshot by the author.

Figure 8: "Beauties pie-slimed WAM (messed with) 5th and final part." A compilation Youtube video by user "TC." A black-and-white video still of a person gasping after their head and shoulders have been covered in thin, gritty slime. Screenshot by the author.

Figure 9: Instagram video from the user "h0nestslimereviews." A black-and-white video still of a left hand with painted nails tracing four impressions through airy, white slime.

Figure 10: "The Raft." From "Creepshow 2." 1987. Michael Gornick, director. A black-and-white film still featuring a dark, oily material that appears to be advancing across the surface of a lake. Screenshot by the author.

Figure 11: "Beauties pie-slimed WAM (messed with) 5th and final part." A compilation Youtube video by user "TC." A black-and-white video still close-up of a person's open mouth, chin and neck after they have been covered in pale slime. Screenshot by the author.

Figure 12: Instagram video from the user "poppingslim3." A black-and-white still of a right hand with shiny, painted nails pressing lightly against a pool of silver, glitter slime. The frame of a "finder" window is visible on either side of the video in the viewer's background. Screenshot by the author.

Figure 13: "The Blob." Yeaworth, Irvin S., director. *The Blob*. Tonylyn Productions, 1958. A black-and-white film still of a very shiny, viscous material that fills an open double doorway of a movie theatre and pushes against the vertical mullion bar dividing the passage. Screenshot by the author.

Figure 14: "The Raft." From "Creepshow 2." 1987. Michael Gornick, director. A black-and-white film still featuring a very glossy, marbled surface that could be bodily gore or manufactured slime. Screenshot by the author.

Figure 15: Instagram video from the user "slim3crunch." A black-and-white still of a left fist squeezing fluffy, white slime. The frame of a "finder" window is visible on either side of the video in the viewer's background. Screenshot by the author.

Figure 16: "The Green Slime." Kinji Fukasaku, director. *The Green Slime.*1968. A black-and-white film still featuring a thin, foaming pool of slime spreading across a white, tiled floor. A medical cot is visible in the image. Files located on the desktop of the viewer's computer are visible to either side of the video. Screenshot by the author.

Figure 17: "You Can't Do That on Television." Nickelodeon, 1999. Geoffrey Darby, director. A black-and-white screenshot of a person wearing a tie, hat and army coat and standing beside a child who has their wrists chained to a gleaming, cave-like wall. Screenshot by the author.

Figure 18: "The Green Slime." Kinji Fukasaku, director. *The Green Slime.* 1968. A black-and-white film still featuring the rough surface of a planet and astronauts in white space suits who are running towards the open door of a spacecraft. Files located on the desktop of the viewer's computer are visible to either side of the video. Screenshot by the author.

Figure 19: "The Raft." From "Creepshow 2." 1987. Michael Gornick, director. A black-and-white film still featuring rippling, dark material floating on the surface of a lake from birds-eye-view. Screenshot by the author.

Figure 20: Instagram video from the user "poppingslim3." A black-and-white still of a hand with manicured nails and tented fingers that are "poking" a pat of marbled slime. Screenshot by the author.

Figure 21: "Girl Slimed in Bathtub." Video no longer available because the account has been terminated. A black-and-white video still of a person sitting on the edge of a bathtub with slime falling down the front of their torso. Files located on the desktop of the viewer's computer are visible to either side of the video. Screenshot by the author.

Figure 22: "The Green Slime." Kinji Fukasaku, director. *The Green Slime*.1968. A black-and-white film still featuring an air vent and a lighted ceiling panel from which a collection of slime is oozing, suspended. Files located on the desktop of the viewer's computer are visible to the right of the video. Screenshot by the author.

Figure 23: "Mud Muse (1968-71)." VernissageTV. A black-and-white video still from "Mud Muse" installed at the MOMA, featuring a close-up of a low, glass trough filled with thin, bubbling mud. Files located on the desktop of the viewer's computer are visible to the right of the video. Screenshot by the author.

Figure 24: "Beauties pie-slimed WAM (messed with) 5th and final part." A compilation Youtube video by user "TC." A black-and-white image of a person gasping after being covered in foamy slime. The framework of a finder window is visible on either side of the video in the viewer's background. Screenshot by the author.

Figure 25: "The Raft." From "Creepshow 2." 1987. Michael Gornick, director. A black-and-white film still featuring the arm and head of a person in a lake opening their mouth and reaching from beneath a dark, web-like blob. Screenshot by the author.

Figure 26: Instagram video from the user "slim3crunch." A black-and-white close-up of the knuckles of a right hand pressing into a pile of fluffy, white slime. Screenshot by the author.

Figure 27: "Beauties pie-slimed WAM (messed with) 5th and final part." A compilation Youtube video by user "TC." A black-and-white image of a femme-presenting person wearing a "Hooters" T-shirt standing in front of a tarp hung on a wall and tilting their head back beneath a stream of opaque slime. The frame of a "finder" window is visible on either side of the video in the viewer's background. Screenshot by the author.

Figure 28: Instagram video from the user "aeslimeic." A black-and-white close-up of the knuckles of a right hand pressing all five fingers into a bowl of dark, glitter slime. Screenshot by the author.

Figure 29: "The Blob." Yeaworth, Irvin S., director. *The Blob.* Tonylyn Productions, 1958. A black-and-white film still featuring the silhouette of a wet hand placed against a surface that is covered with transparent slime. Screenshot by the author.

Figure 30: "Girl Slimed in Bathtub." Youtube video no longer available because the account associated has been terminated. A black-and-white video still of a femme-presenting person smiling as white slime runs down their hair and face. Screenshot by the author.

Figure 31: Instagram video from the user "h0nestslimereviews." A black-and-white video still of a left hand with painted nails tracing four impressions through airy, white slime. The frame of a "finder" window is visible on either side of the video in the viewer's background. Screenshot by the author.

Figure 32: "The Green Slime." Kinji Fukasaku, director. *The Green Slime.*1968. A black-and-white film still featuring a thin, foaming pool of slime spreading out on a white floor. A medical cot is visible in the image. Files located on the desktop of the viewer's computer are visible to either side of the video. Screenshot by the author.

Figure 33: Instagram video from the user "aeslimeic." A black-and-white close-up of the knuckles of a left hand pressing four fingers into a mass of smooth slime. The frame of a "finder" window is visible on either side of the video in the viewer's background. Screenshot by the author.

Figure 34: "MESS EM UP GOOD! A Messy Montage. TOO extreme for live action!" A compilation Youtube video by user "3D Slimer." A black-and-white video still featuring an animated, femme-presenting figure holding both palms forward while being "slimed" head-on. Screenshot by the author.

Figure 35: "MESS EM UP GOOD! A Messy Montage. TOO extreme for live action!" A compilation Youtube video by user "3D Slimer." A black-and-white video still featuring an animated, femme-presenting figure confined to a chair while being "slimed" via mechanized hoses. Screenshot by the author.

Figure 36: "The Raft." From "Creepshow 2." 1987. Michael Gornick, director. A black-and-white film still featuring oily, dark material floating on the surface of a lake. Screenshot by the author.

Figure 37: "MESS EM UP GOOD! A Messy Montage. TOO extreme for live action!" A compilation Youtube video by user "3D Slimer." A black-and-white video still featuring an animated, femme-presenting figure assuming a posture of surprise while being "slimed" via mechanized hoses. Screenshot by the author.

Figure 38: "The Green Slime." Kinji Fukasaku, director. *The Green Slime*.1968. A black-and-white film still featuring an air vent and a lighted ceiling panel from which a collection of slime is oozing, suspended. Files located on the desktop of the viewer's computer are visible to the right of the video. Screenshot by the author.

Figure 39: "The Blob." Yeaworth, Irvin S., director. *The Blob*. Tonylyn Productions, 1958. A black-and-white film still of a very shiny, viscous material that fills an open double doorway of a movie theatre and pushes against the vertical mullion bar in the center of the doorway. Screenshot taken by the author.

Figure 40: "Beauties pie-slimed WAM (messed with) 5th and final part." A compilation Youtube video by user "TC." A black-and-white image of a femme with long hair gasping while being "slimed" from above. The framework of a "finder" window is visible on either side of the video in the viewer's background. Screenshot by the author.

Figure 41: "You Can't Do That on Television." Nickelodeon, 1999. Geoffrey Darby, director. A black-and-white screenshot of a masculine-presenting adult wearing a tie, hat and army coat and standing beside a child with wrists chained to a shiny wall. Red and green boxes appear at the bottom of the image. Screenshot by the author.

Figure 42: "Beauties pie-slimed WAM (messed with) 5th and final part." A compilation Youtube video by user "TC." A black-and-white image of a person standing in front of a tarp beneath a stream of opaque slime. The frame of a "finder" window is visible to the right side of the video, in the viewer's background. Screenshot by the author.

Figure 43: Instagram video from the user "poppingslim3." A black-and-white still of two hands with tented fingers "poking" a pat of opaque slime. Screenshot by the author.

Figure 44: "The Green Slime." Kinji Fukasaku, director. *The Green Slime.*1968. A black-and-white film still featuring the rough surface of a planet and an astronaut in a white space suit running towards the open door of a spacecraft. Screenshot by the author.

Figure 45: "The Raft." From "Creepshow 2." 1987. Michael Gornick, director. A black-and-white film still featuring a very shiny, marbled surface appears to be either gore or slime. Screenshot by the author.

Figure 46: "MESS EM UP GOOD! A Messy Montage. TOO extreme for live action!" A compilation Youtube video by user "3D Slimer." A black-and-white video still featuring an animated, femme-presenting figure bent forward and open-mouthed after being "slimed." Screenshot by the author.

Figure 47: "The Green Slime." Kinji Fukasaku, director. *The Green Slime.*1968. A black-and-white film still featuring the hands and knees of an astronaut who is wearing a white space suit and bending to pick up a tool covered in green slime. Screenshot by the author.

Figure 48: "Beauties pie-slimed WAM (messed with) 5th and final part." A compilation Youtube video by user "TC." Screenshot taken by the author. A black-and-white video still close-up of a femme-presenting person's open mouth, chin and neck just after they have been covered in slime. Screenshot by the author.

Select Works Cited

Adamczak, Bini. Sophie Lewis, translator. "On
    Circlusion." *Mask Magazine*. July 2016.

Anderson, Antje Schaum. "Gendered Pleasure,
    Gendered Plot: Defloration as Climax in
    "Clarissa" and "Memoirs of a Woman of
    Pleasure." *The Journal of Narrative Technique*
    25.2, 1995.

Bataille, Georges, et al. *Visions of Excess: Selected
    Writings, 1927-1939*. University of Minnesota
    Press, 2017.

Bellamy, Dodie. *The Barf Manifesto*. Ugly Duckling Press,
    2008.

Cleland, John. *Fanny Hill: Memoirs of a Woman of
    Pleasure*. Penguin, 1985.

Corliss, William R. *Handbook of Unusual Natural
    Phenomena*. Gramercy, 1995.

Daley, Jason. "Medieval Manuscripts Are a DNA
    Smorgasbord." *Smithsonian.com*, Smithsonian
    Institution, 31 July 2017.

Lange-Berndt, Petra. *Materiality*. MIT Press: Whitechapel:
    Documents of Contemporary Art, 2015.

McRoy, Jay, '"Parts Is Parts": Pornography, Splatter
    Film and the Politics of Corporeal
    Disintegration', in Ian Conrich (ed.), *Horror
    Zone: The Cultural Experience of
    Contemporary Horror Cinema*. London: I.B.
    Tauris, 2014. Print.

Poole, W. Scott. *Monsters in America: Our Historical
    Obsession with the Hideous and the Haunting*.
    Baylor University Press, 2018.

Rebekah J. Kowal, "Blurp, Blap, Blop: Rebekah Kowel Listens in on Robert Rauschenberg's Mude Muse." *Art Orbit #3* Sept, 1998. http://artnode.se/artorbit/issue3/f_merge/f_merge.html

Welchman, John C. Mike Kelly: *Minor Histories: Statements, Conversations, Proposals.* MIT Press, 2004.

Williams, Linda. "Fetishism and Hard Core: Marx, Freud, and "The Money Shot." In *Hard Core: Power, Pleasure, and the "frenzy of the Visible".* Berkeley: University of California Press, 1989. Print.

Wulff, Winifred. *Rosa Anglica Sev Rosa Medicin Johannis Anglici: an Early Modern Irish Translation of a Section of the Mediaeval Medical Text-Book of John of Gaddesden.* Nabu Press, 2010.

Acknowledgements

The writing and research for this project was supported by a three-month Independent Research Grant to Iceland through the American-Scandinavian Foundation and by a fellowship to the Vermont Studio Center. Thank you to Noam Dorr, Marianne Templeton, Phoebe Stubbs, and Mimi Cabell for trips over land and into hot waters farther north. Additional writing and research was conducted at the Museum of Water and the Volcano Museum in Stykkishólmur, at the National Library of Iceland in Reykjavìk, at the Gund Library at the Cleveland Institute of Art and the Kelvin Smith Library at Case Western University in Cleveland. Thank you to Nicole Walker, Rúnar Helgi Vignisson, and the NonfictioNow organizers. Special thanks to Miriam Intrator and Michele Jennings of Ohio University Special Collections, and to Nikki Woods of the Reinberger Gallery for support of this project, which appeared in interactive, tactile installations in 2019. Thank you to Lisa Peters of Case Western for your consultation on many drippy images.

Thank you to my editor, Emily Kiernan, whose insights encouraged clarity and play in this manuscript, and to the editorial team at Noemi Press including Carmen Giménez Smith, Evan Lavender-Smith, Sarah Gzemski, Suzi F. Garcia, and Emily Alex.

My thanks and admiration to Birgitta, Martin, and Eydis, fellows in lanolin. Unending gratitude to my mother, Meg, who has forever bothered me with monks, books of skin, and origins of language. Thank you to Eric LeMay for being a guiding light. I am grateful to Sarah Rose Nordgren, Piper Lane, Nina Boutsikaris, Julia Conrad, Mary Kate Hurley, Dinty W. Moore, Courtney Kessel and Bianca Spriggs for early feedback on this manuscript. To my colleagues, Jonathan Rosati, Barry Underwood, and Tina Cassara, thank you for guidance through early installation work. Thanks to Rich Levinson and Nao Mizuno for conversations about sound design. Thank you to my students at the Cleveland Institute of Art, who inspire and teach me every day.

I am especially grateful to Susanna Hempstead, Christine Adams, Georgia Flaum, Morgen Sedlacek, Zoë Bossiere, Andrew Dietz, Hilary Plum, Zach Savich, Caryl Pagel, and Meg Wade for their friendship and conversation.

To Tommy Mira y Lopez, patient and hilarious, thank you for earliest encouragements and finalmost edits.